Wishford Station

Stations of the GWR No.2

Terry Waldron

Acknowledgements

I would like to thank all the local people who I have talked to, they have given me many leads to follow up on, there are too many to be listed individually but I must single out Kevin Regan who has assisted at records offices, given me many leads to follow, provided information from his own research and has read and commented on each chapter of this book as it has developed over the years. Staff at local libraries (Salisbury, Warminster, Bath) and record offices (PRO, WSRO, English Heritage, Swindon Steam Archive, Bristol) have pointed me in the right direction within their archives and produced very quickly the large volume of documentation that has needed to be read. Finally I must thank the Signalling Record Society for their advice on signalling matters and members of the GW Study Group who have given me information from their own collections.

All photos the author, except: Cover, 8352 on a down coal, Diesel Railcar No1., 8327 hauls a rake of LSWR and SR coaches, 4387 heads the down 0812 Bristol to Southampton, 3376 heads a passenger train, SR 1625, 5969 Honington Hall. Endpiece - HC Casserly; Front cover - John Alsop; A class 33 on a down train - Chris Nevard; Wilfred Talbot - Colin Maggs. p47 & p53 West/Cannings Family Collection. Title page: STEAM - Museum of the GWR, Swindon.

Website - www.BretwaldaBooks.com
Twitter - @Bretwaldabooks
Facebook - Bretwalda Books
Blog - bretwaldabooks.blogspot.co.uk/

Bretwalda Books
Unit 8, Fir Tree Close, Epsom,
Surrey KT17 3LD
info@BretwaldaBooks.com
www.BretwaldaBooks.com
ISBN 978-1-909099-71-5

CONTENTS

Foreword   4

Chapter 1   Wishford Railway Station   5

Chapter 2   Trackwork and Platforms   24

Chapter 3   The Signal Box and Timetables   33

Chapter 4   Trains   38

Chapter 5   Station Master's House and Staff   44

Chapter 6   Sidings and Freight   51

Chapter 7   Use of Land After Closure   62

About the Author   64

FOREWORD

It was an advertisement in the local Parish Magazine asking for information on Wishford Station that lead to my first meeting with Terry Waldron in The Royal Oak pub in Wishford a few years ago. Since then Terry has searched archives, talked to many who remember the station and found out through timetables and photographs so much about Wishford Station it is good now that all this can be put together. Wishford like the other stations in the Wylye valley played an important part in rural life and the fact that 58 years since its closure there are still people who remember using it to go to school, work, holidays and collecting all sorts of merchandise from the goods depot. Milk and coal merchants, building materials and race horses all came by rail. During World War Two although not as busy as Wylye station, Wishford did play its part for the nearby American camp at Grovely wood. The heyday was probably in the late 1920s and through the 1930s when the variety of locomotives that could be seen through Wishford was huge, 4-4-0s Badminton and Bulldogs with such names as Beesborough , Gooch, Dominion of Canada, 4-6-0 Star and Saint class, Halls and Castles. On the freight side everything from outside frame Aberdare 2-6-0s 43xx 2-6-0s through to 28xx 2-8-0s and the Heavy Freight 72xx 2-8-2 Tanks. Wishford also saw steam rail motors and the early A.E.C. Diesel railcars. Sadly the station and all others in the valley passed into Southern Region hands in September 1950 and after that the writing was on the wall. Closed in 1955 just as the population of all the villages was on the increase. Now for those many that work in Salisbury, Trowbridge, Chippenham, Bath and Bristol there is only the car along the congested A36.

Kevin M Regan

Previous page: SR 1625, one of the two regular SR locos that could be seen on the line, hauling Portsmouth to Bristol trains.

CHAPTER 1
WISHFORD RAILWAY STATION

Great Wishford is a small Wiltshire village set in the Wylye Valley, between the river Wylye on the eastern side and Grovely Woods on the western side and at the foot of the chalk downs. . Many houses are built of stone and flint, or brick and flint and many with attractive thatched roofs.

The railway follows the river through much of the valley. The village is set in agricultural land, much of which belongs to the Wilton Estate (Earl Pembroke). The village is steeped in history, being reported in the Doomsday Book and has a 400 year old tradition of Oak Apple Day, (dating back to 1603) where villagers celebrate their rights of collection of firewood from Grovely Woods. In the church

44932 powers away from the outskirts of Great Wishford on a Bath and Bristol Christmas Special on 25/11/2010.

5

of St Giles is a hand pump, fire engine, bought for the village in 1728 and remained in use until the 1920's.

In the north east wall of the churchyard are set breadstones telling the price of bread from 1800.

History of the Line

Roger Hopkins and Sons, a Bath Engineer, surveyed much of Wiltshire, Somerset and Dorset for The Bath and Weymouth Great Western Union Railway in 1836 (with one branch terminating at Warminster). Plans of the line exist in both Wiltshire and Somerset Records Offices, these are extensive and also show who owned each plot of land the line would pass through. In addition there are reports in the Salisbury and Winchester Journal on a number of dates in 1836.

Roger Hopkins also did a preliminary survey for The Salisbury and Warminster Railway, the Salisbury and Warminster Journal reports on 18 April 1836:

"To effect a junction with the South Western and Portsmouth, Salisbury and Southampton Railways and the Bath and Weymouth Great Western Union Railway at Warminster.

Prospectus will be issued in a few days containing the names of a Provisional Committee and the cost and revenue of undertaking.

8352 on a down coal from Aberdare on 14/9/1936. Taken at Stockton Dairy Farm Bridge (ST973385) and heading for Salisbury.

The line of the Railway will afford a cheap and expeditious communication with the Somersetshire Collieries, from which coals are now supplied by land carriage, with Bristol, the railways and places above mentioned, and will in effect unite the two channels and the Eastern and Western Coasts of England. It is confidently expected that the undertaking will prove a source of convenience to the public and immense profit to Capitalists.

Hodding & Everett, Solicitors Salisbury

T H Griffith, Solicitor Warminster

April 13 1836."

And again on May 2 1836

"Salisbury and Weymouth Railway

To effect a junction with the South Western and Hampshire and Wiltshire Railways at or near to Salisbury and the Bath & Weymouth Great Western Union Railway at Warminster.

A preliminary survey of this line has been carried out by Messrs. Hopkins and

---

CHRONOLOGICAL DATES FOR THE STATION

Open to freight 11 June 1856
Open to passenger 30 June 1856
Track converted from Broad Gauge 19 June 1874
Passing loop at Wishford 1898
Double track operational 28 April 1901
Additional sidings September 1909
Regional Boundary change BR(WR) to (SR) September 1950
Last train 17 September 1955
Formally Closed 19 September 1955
Sidings taken out of use 27 November 1955
Footbridge removed c1958
Sidings removed 10 September 1961
Station buildings removed c1963
Platform faces removed c1963
Signal box non operational 26 August 1964
Signal box removed c1964
Station Master's House sold 1976
Goods shed removed c1983

Sons, prospectus will be ready for delivery on Monday, the 9th May at the offices of Messrs Swain, Stevens & Co, 6 Fredericks Place, Old Jewry; R E Smith Esq. 3 New Beswell Court, Lincolns Inn; Messrs Mant & Bruce, 2 Wood Street Bath and the offices of the solicitors.

Hodding & Everett, Salisbury
T H Griffith, Warminster
Salisbury 29 April 1836"

Followed on May 30 1836 by:

"A meeting of landowners and others opposed to the line of Rail Road from Salisbury to Warminster will be held at the Deptford Inn on Weds 1st June at 12 o'clock".

Then, on May 30 1836, it was reported that the Salisbury and Warminster Railway had a capital of £200,000 in 400 shares £50 each. Deposit £2 per share. (Author's note: £50 in 1836 would be equivalent to £2,300 in 2013) This reference lists the 11 members of the Provisional Committee, the Bankers and the Solicitors.

On June 6 1836 came the following statement:

"Deptford Inn Wilts 1 June 1836.

At a meeting of Landowners & others residing or possessing property on or near the projected line of railroad from Salisbury to Warminster.

It was resolved that the proposed railroad from Salisbury to Warminster appeared to be wholly uncalled for by the Traffic of either of those places, or of the immediate district, and that such an undertaking would prove seriously detrimental to the Agricultural interests of the neighborhood, and they pledged themselves to each other to give every opposition to the same. It was also ordered that so much of their Resolution be inserted in the County Papers.

The undernamed by themselves or Agents attended and signed the Resolution to such effect.

William Temple, Esquire, Chairman."

This reference listed 47 attendees of which 5 were Clergy.

On June 13 1836 it is recorded:

"Salisbury and Warminster Railway

With a view to guard the Public against misrepresentation and artful insinuation the Committee of this Railway condescended to notice an advertisement put forth by the London and Exeter...

In reference to the powerful opposition of Landed Proprietors which was 'Organized' at the Deptford Inn this Committee fearlessly assert that

8

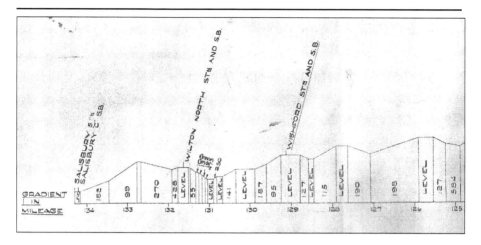

The gradient profile for the line from Salisbury as built.

notwithstanding the bold assumption contained in the resolution of this 'Organized' opposition, many of the gentlemen under whose name it appears are not landowners of any property within miles of the line proposed by this Committee.

A prospectus of this Railway has been long before the Public. The principles on which its calculations are founded have been rigidly scrutinized and generally approved; its advantages to the Public are so evident and certain that this Committee cannot be induced by mere sinister objections or in their determination to perfect an undertaking so auspiciously commenced.

Hodding & Everett, T H Griffith, Solicitors June 10 1836."

Unfortunately the Resolution cannot be found in the Salisbury and Winchester Journal during June or July of 1836 and this paper remains silent on the proposed Railway thereafter. No plans of the survey by Roger Hopkins can be found but within the listing of persons who signed the Resolution there are at least two who resided in Steeple Langford (I have been unable to find their precise address to establish whether they were or were not landowners in the vicinity of the proposed railway) and thus it can reasonably be assumed that the line proposed from Warminster to Salisbury must be very close to the line that was eventually built (and is still in existence, and in daily use).

Isambard Brunel submitted a scheme on 9 June 1844 to interested parties at a meeting in the Bath Arms, Warminster, for a single track Broad Gauge (7ft 0 ¼ inches) line from Thingley (between Bath and Chippenham) to Weymouth with a branch to Salisbury (this line being converted to standard gauge of 4ft 8 ½ ins. on 18 and 19 June 1874).

The following comes from the Directors Minute Book:

Warminster 9 July 1844

Mr. Brunel submitted to the meeting plans and surveys prepared by him showing the direction of the intended line and he explained fully the views which he entertained of the mode in which the railway should be constructed and carried for the benefit of public traffic and for local advantages of the towns etc. having due regard to the interests and convenience of the owners and occupiers of land throughout the whole of it.

The length of the direct line from Thingly near Corsham to Salisbury was represented to be 37 ½ miles.

From Melksham to Devizes 7 miles

From Staverton to Bradford 2 miles

From Westbury to Frome 5 miles.

The addition of a single Coal Branch line from Frome to Radstock would be 8 miles – if this is considered a desirable measure to adopt in conjunction with the other Passenger lines of the Railway. Mr. Brunel represented that as far as he could judge at present from information already obtained the sum of £650,000 (equivalent to £33,000,000 in 2011) would be fully adequate to cover every expense in forming the Company, obtaining the Act, and in completing all purchases, constructing the works and Permanent Way upon the whole distance including the Coal Branch to Radstock.

After full discussion of the subject it was resolved:

That it was expedient now to form a Provisional Committee for the purpose of carrying out the important objects submitted to this meeting on the conditions proposed by the Great Western Railway Co. Walter Long Esq. MP was requested to accept the office of Chairman of the Provisional Committee to which he expressed his assent.

Trowbridge 3 Feb 1846

The Secretary reported that he had attended a meeting with Mr. Phelps and Mr. R Ward and Mr. Saunders, Secretary to the GWR Co., on the subject of various preliminary arrangements for the purchase of land on the Salisbury Branch and that all was now ready for the serving of notices and for the Land Agent to commence his operations.

The Wilts, Somerset and Weymouth Railway (WS&WR) was formed and had an Act of Parliament passed for this line on 30 June 1845 and construction began with Brunel as the Engineer. An extract from this Act reads:

XXVI. And be it enacted, That the first-mentioned of such Railways shall commence by a Junction with the Line of the Great Western Railway at or near Thingley in the Parish of Corsham in the County of Wilts, and shall pass through the following Places; (that is to say,) Corsham, Laycock, Melksham, Broughton Gifford, Holt, Bradford, Trowbridge, North Bradley, Westbury, Upton Scudamore, Warminster, Bishopstrow, Norton Bavant, Sutton Veny, Heytesbury, Knook, Upton Lovell, Boyton, Codford St. Peter, Sherrington, Stockton, Fisherton-de-la-Mere, Wily, Steeple Langford, Little Langford, Great Wishford, South Newton, Wilton, Fugglestone St. Peter, Bemerton and Fisherton Anger, partly within the City of New Sarum, all in the County of Wilts, and shall terminate within the said city of New Sarum near Fisherton Gaol in the said Parish of Fisherton Anger.

XL. And it be enacted, That in making the said Railway it shall be lawful for the Company to cross Roads numbered on the Plans as herein-after mentioned on the Level thereof; that is to say,

In the Parish of Great Wishford the Road numbered 16; in the Parish of Wily the road numbered 38; in the Parish of Codford St. Peter the Roads numbered 10 and 27 respectively; in the Parish of Upton Lovell the Roads numbered 7 and 15 respectively; ....

At the time of the Act in 1845 a map shows the line going through Wishford but NOT showing a station.

A total of 12 acres and 24 roods of land were acquired to build the line (apparently sufficient to build the later proposed station as no further purchases of land can be found) through the parish of Wishford, the majority of the land was owned by The Earl of Pembroke (much of which was let out to villagers as pasture and arable land) and Reverend F De Viel Williams (draft agreements for purchase of land being laid before the board on 4 March 1843).

The original junction between the Salisbury Branch and the Weymouth line was to have been at Upton Scudamore, a Supplement to The Act was put in place in 1846 to change this to Westbury.

Within the Tender Information for Contractors there was a clause –"they were to co-operate in preventing Sunday labour in every instance when not of actual and indispensible necessity" and "bind themselves not to pay workmen at beer shops or public houses".

Contractors for the line were:

Melksham Contract - John Pritchard

Devizes Contract - H & C Blandford

Bath Contract - Messrs Tredwell

Trowbridge Contract - Matthew Craufurd

Warminster Contract - Matthew Craufurd

Salisbury Contract - Matthew Craufurd

Frome Contract - Messrs Roach and Pildritch

As a result of the large amount of 'navvies' that would be working on the line the Chief Constable of Wiltshire, Captain Meredith, recommended an increase of 6 men to his force.

The railway continued to be built when the section from Westbury to Warminster was opened on 9 September 1851 as single track Broad Gauge. It was a further 5 years before the section from Warminster to Salisbury was completed (also single track broad gauge). Mineral (mainly coal) traffic (probably from the Radstock coalfields) started running on 11 June 1856 and the line was formally opened to passenger traffic on 30 June 1856.

The delay in opening the whole line was due to the difficulty in obtaining funding at reasonable rates during mid 1847 and as thus no new contracts were let and existing contracts were reduced and later stopped completely. This left, in many areas, bridges and earthworks unfinished. Purchase of land was postponed with some land being left in the hands of its previous owners.

In early 1850 when the GWR essentially took over the WS&WR they offered original shareholders 4% guaranteed stock in lieu of their shares (the takeover was formalized in 1851). At the end of this year the Committee of Consultation (who were looking into the affairs of the GWR) strongly recommended to the shareholders that the line should not be extended beyond Frome and Warminster. This proved unpopular locally (despite the depositions of the previously proposed railway in 1836) and many committees were formed to induce the Company to complete their original undertakings. In view of the GWR Directors appearing to not wish to listen to their pleas they took legal proceedings to compel them to complete the unfinished portions, and petitions were presented to Parliament.

The Mayor of Salisbury went before the Caldwell Committee in 1853 and part of his evidence suggested that the GWR would prefer to carry passengers from Bristol to Portsmouth and Southampton via Reading and Basingstoke as this gave them a higher ticket revenue.

A debate in the House of Lords on 10 June 1853 ran as follows

The MARQUESS of BATH presented a petition from Salisbury and certain parishes in Wiltshire, praying the House to grant no further powers to the Great Western Railway Company till they shall have completed the line between Warminster and Salisbury. The noble Marquess said that the inhabitants of the district complained of the non-completion of this line, in consequence of which they were prevented from getting coals at a comparatively cheap rate from the north of England. The Great Western Railway Company, whose conduct in this matter had been marked throughout by a selfish jealousy, had obtained a Bill for the line, not with any intention of constructing it, but simply with the view of preventing the South Western Railway Company from encroaching on what they considered to be their own territory, and having got the Bill they now refused to make the line. Nor was this a local grievance merely, but a question of national importance; for the line, if completed, would considerably shorten the distance between Bristol and Portsmouth—a circumstance of great importance in case of a necessity arising for conveying troops from one place to the other at a short notice. A great principle was involved in this question, illustrating as it did the

A British Railways Britannia Class locomotive approaching Wishford. This class of locomotives was built from 1951 to haul express passenger trains.

iniquitous conduct and bad faith of the Great Western Railway Company. The Petitioners before appealing to Parliament had endeavoured to obtain legal redress; and subsequently a deputation from them had waited on the President of the Board of Trade, and on the noble Earl at the head of the Government; but in both instances they had failed in getting relief. He (the Marquess of Bath) now wished to ask if Her Majesty's Government were prepared to make any inquiry into the case; and, if so, whether they would use their influence to prevent any further powers being granted to the Great Western Railway Company until the result of that inquiry should be made public? and, in case the Government were not prepared to institute any inquiry, he hoped that at all events they would not offer any opposition to a proposal for withholding the grant of any further powers to the Great Western Company until they should give some guarantee for the completion of this line.

LORD STANLEY OF ALDERLEY said, that this was one of a great many cases in which no doubt great inconvenience resulted to the public from railway mismanagement. It was well known that the law had decided that there was no power to compel railway companies to perform their contracts; and, therefore, he was afraid that Government could take no measures to enforce the fulfilment of these obligations. To make an ex post facto law, might have the effect of bearing hard upon other parties. Such a law might be all very well in a case like the present; but if they applied it to one case, they must apply it to all. With regard, however, to the future, the feeling of Government had been sufficiently shown by their proposing the Sessional order, which had been applied to every Railway Bill which had come before the House of Commons this Session, and which required that in the case of any railway company already in existence, and paying dividends, asking powers to construct a new line, they should be compelled to construct it within a given time under the penalty of having their dividends suspended; and that in the case of a railway company not paying dividends asking such powers, they should be called upon to pay down a deposit, which should be left in the hands of Government, and in the event of the Company not fulfilling their engagement it was provided that the deposit should be forfeited to the Consolidated Fund. It was also intended that this Sessional order should be continued in future years. With regard to the future, then, it would thus be seen that Government had taken such steps as were necessary for compelling railway companies to complete their contracts. With respect to the inconvenience which the non-completion of the railway in question occasioned to the districts of country in which it was situated, he was far from disputing that it must be very great. He would only call the attention of the noble Marquess to the fact that the powers which were granted to the Great Western Company in 1847, expired in 1854; so that next year it would be open to a new company to apply for powers to effect the works, if the Great Western Company should still decline to continue them. Under these circumstances, he did not see that the Government could interfere at all in the matter. If it should be the opinion of Parliament, or of a Committee of cither House, that it would be expedient to refuse any further powers to the Great Western Company until they had completed the lines they had already commenced, it was for them so to decide.

LORD CAMPBELL said, it might be useful for their Lordships to know the existing state of the law on this subject. It had formerly been thought obligatory on railway companies to make the lines for which they had obtained powers, inasmuch as they got possession of the land and interfered with public rights; and a mandamus was accordingly granted by the Court of Queen's Bench to compel the construction of a line so contracted to be made. There had recently, however, been a decision in the Exchequer Chamber which set aside the judgment of the Queen's Bench, and determined that there was no power to issue a mandamus to compel a railway company to complete a line for which they had obtained an Act of Parliament. From that judgment there would be an appeal to their Lordships' House, and they would have to decide between the Court of Queen's Bench and the Exchequer Chamber.

The BISHOP of SALISBURY said, the principle which had been laid down by the noble Marquess that this great company should not be permitted to obtain any Bill for a new undertaking till they had completed those which they had already begun, appeared to him so plain and just a principle that he could hardly conceive it should not weigh both their Lordships and the House of Commons.

The EARL of MALMESBURY could not see any hardship in the course proposed by his noble Friend. The company had made a contract with Parliament and the public, and they had been empowered to raise money on the faith of it, which money they had spent for different objects from those they undertook to carry out, He thought his noble Friend had scarcely placed in a sufficiently strong light the great public importance of uniting, by railway communication, the Irish and the English Channel, and thus affording facilities for the conveyance of troops to any given part of the south and north-western coast. At present there was a distance of about forty-five miles on the south coast, or two days' march for troops, between Dorchester and Exeter, which was without any railway. He begged to lay on the table a petition from Salisbury, praying their Lordships not to empower the Great Western Company to make any new works until they had concluded those which had been referred to by his noble Friend.

LORD REDESDALE said, he believed the reason why the Great Western Railway Company had not completed that line between Warminster and Salisbury was, that a great many travellers would pass over it to Salisbury, and then proceed on to London by the South-Western Railway, instead of going round to Bath, and from Bath to London by the Great Western Railway, according to the existing arrangement. The fact was, that no efficient control could at present be exercised over the proceedings of railway companies; and he trusted that the eyes of Parliament would at length be opened to the necessity of conferring a controlling power in that matter upon some duly constituted public body. He believed that the Great Western Railway Company had money enough to construct that line, or any works of a similar character. He had himself demanded from that company a statement of their capital, but he had not yet received that statement; and until it should be furnished to him, he would not allow any Bills of this Company to be proceeded with.

Petition ordered to lie on the table.

The lawsuits were successfully defeated with the exception of the branch from Bathampton to Bradford on Avon for which its completion was made absolute by the Queen's Bench in the Michaelmus Term after a Trial in the Somerset

The Wishford Station sign, showing bridge rail supports for the Running in Board (GWR terminology for Station Nameboard).

Assizes. The GWR Directors reconsidered the whole case and promoted a Bill for an extension of time to complete the unfinished work, this eventually became an Act of Parliament on 31 July 1854.

The Salisbury and Winchester Journal of 16 February 1856:

Extract from a Report of the Special Committee on the affairs of the Company:

The next large expenditure is that of the Wilts Somerset and Weymouth Railway of which 31 ½ miles are open viz. Thingley Junction to Frome 19 miles; Westbury to Warminster 4 ½ miles; the portion still to be opened Frome to Weymouth 54 miles; Warminster to Salisbury 20 ½ miles; Bradford to Bathampton.

The Salisbury and Winchester Journal 5 July 1856 p3

Opening of the Wilts, Somerset and Weymouth Railway

The Salisbury and Warminster branch of this line was opened on Monday last, but without any of the formalities which are usual on those occasions. The first train left Fisherton Station about 40 minutes after 6 o'clock, and a large number of persons assembled to witness its departure. We are informed that considerable interest was felt throughout the line, and that numerous persons assembled at the various stations to witness the passing of the trains. The engine was dressed with evergreen and flowers, and at some of the stations flags were displayed. The first train arrived at Fisherton shortly after eleven o'clock, a very large number of persons being assembled at the Station. There were four trains to and from this city during the day, most of which were filled. The permanent way, in consequence of the length of time which has been occupied in construction, is thoroughly consolidated, and this together with the peculiar mode of laying rails on the Great Western line, causes the propulsion of the train to be unattended with that oscillation which is so unpleasant on some of the narrow gauge lines. The line is some 20 miles long, and there are six intermediate stations between Salisbury and Warminster. It passes through a valley remarkable for its fertility, and the diversity of its scenery in some parts of the line is remarkably picturesque. The opening of this line will be the means of bringing the extensive coal fields of Somersetshire into closer proximity with this city, and also with the important port of Southampton and the great naval arsenal of Portsmouth, in which places for a long time past, prices have ranged high in consequence of the great demand for coals for the purpose of steam navigation. The terminus, which is within half a mile of the Cathedral, is well constructed, being in fact an ornament to the place; and all the other stations on the line are substantial buildings, well constructed and of suitable dimensions for a large amount of traffic. The line has been opened just one month earlier than the time stipulated in the Act of Parliament. The Wilts, Somerset and Weymouth, however, will not be finished until the connecting link from Tilehurst to Reading is ready for opening, which will be within a few months from this date. The whole branches and extensions of the system (excepting, perhaps, the narrow gauge to Basingstoke) will then have been brought into working operation, and the outlay on the undertaking concluded. There are 72 ½ miles of this line still unopened, viz., Frome to Weymouth, 54 miles; Devizes Branch, 8 ½; Bradford to Bathampton, 10 miles. On the whole we have little doubt that the opening of this line to this city will be productive of great advantages to the inhabitants of this locality.

When the line initially opened the whole branch from Westbury to Salisbury was worked by a single needle telegraph.

The first day of formal passenger traffic was on 30 June 1856, this being

3376 heads a passenger train on 19/7/1937 taken at the approaches to Heytesbury.

preceded by freight trains running from 11 June 1856 and a special inspection train on 19 June 1856. This latter train was for the Government Inspector, Col. Yolland, who was accompanied by the Resident Engineer, Mr Ward, a number of Great Western Railway Company officials and invited ladies and gentlemen. They were met at Salisbury Terminus by a large number of spectators who all cheered when the train entered the station. The official party had a luncheon at the station before returning at 5 o'clock. At the time it was stated the line would open in a week or two.

The line was converted from Broad Gauge to Standard Gauge during the period 16 to 19 June 1874. Some 2000 men working around 18 hours per day were used. At the time of the conversion there was a one day abstention from work at some of the Radstock Pits because they feared lack of work and therefore loss of wages, the management got them back to work by explaining the coal mined would be stacked until it could be again transported by rail.

The Warminster Herald of 20 June 1874 reports:

"The Somerset Coalfield

On Monday three of the largest of Countess Waldegraves pits at Radstock were suddenly laid idle. During the present week many of the markets which are supplied from these pits closed, in consequence of the liability of the Great Western Railway Company to carry minerals on their Salisbury and Weymouth lines, which during the week will be changed from broad to narrow gauge. It was explained to the men by Mr. McMurtle that work would be found for them, and the coal would be stacked. To this arrangement the men at meetings held by them objected, and on Monday laid the pits idle by abstaining from work. We have heard that the men agreed to return to work Tuesday morning, but should the above conduct be repeated immediate legal proceedings will be taken against the men, it being illegal to cease work in such a way."

Initially there was only one passing loop that being at Wylye (where trains could take water), further passing loops were built at Wilton in 1867, Heytesbury in 1888, Codford in 1898 and Wishford in 1898. Conversion to double track took place from Wylye to Wishford on 3 March 1901 and from Wishford to Wilton on 28 April of that year.

Although the line still operates today all of the village stations are now closed (except Dilton Marsh between Warminster and Westbury), with no stations existing between Warminster and Salisbury.

On 18 January 1955 the District Traffic Superintendent, Woking, Surrey

(British Transport Commission, British Railways, Southern Region) issued a letter to The Clerk Salisbury Rural District Council stating:

The economic circumstances of stations between Salisbury and Warminster, i.e. Wilton North, Wishford, Wylye, Codford, Heytesbury have been under review, and as a result the conclusion has been arrived at that in view of the very small passenger usage the train service at them is not justified, and that the amount of freight traffic dealt with at Wishford and Heytesbury does not warrant their retention.

It is proposed, therefore, to close Wishford and Heytesbury entirely, and to withdraw the passenger train service from Wilton North, Wylye and Codford.

This letter established that current bus services adequately covered the travel needs in the area. It also talked about current freight collection and delivery by motors. Further correspondence in February 1955 established the Financial details and that these closures would result in a saving:

Minimum gross estimated savings £5,300

Estimated loss of receipts £1,300

Net improvement in revenue £4,000

A traffic service census carried out in 1954 showed the following daily average passenger traffic (stations Wilton North to Heytesbury), where times are departing Salisbury:

7.25 Salisbury to Bristol 7 joined, 2 alighted

A class 33 on a down train passing the disused goods shed in 1982

9.34 Portsmouth to Bristol 0 joined, 0 alighted

12.45 Portsmouth to Weston Super Mare 1 joined, 2 alighted

4.18 Portsmouth to Bristol 0 joined, 2 alighted (request stop Wylye)

5.02 Salisbury to Bristol 0 joined, 7 alighted

This resulted in 59 stops where NO passengers joined or alighted. Average daily total passengers for Wishford were 2 joined and 2 alighted

Times departing Westbury

7.18 Swindon to Salisbury 4 joined, 0 alighted

9.28 Bristol to Portsmouth 3 joined, 2 alighted

11.45 Bristol to Portsmouth 2 joined, 0 alighted

4.20 Bradford on Avon to Codford 0 Joined, 1 alighted

5.44 Bristol to Portsmouth 1 joined, 2 alighted

8.33 Bristol to Eastleigh 2 joined, 2 alighted

This resulting in 89 stops where NO passengers joined or alighted. Average daily, total, passengers for Wishford were 2 joined and 1 alighted. Freight for Wishford for the whole year showed 146 (full or part full) wagons sent out and 470 (full or part full) wagons received in, Heytesbury fared much worse with 9 wagons out and 75 wagons received.

The Salisbury Journal Friday 25 February 1955

WYLYE VALLEY RAILWAY SERVICE

British Railways proposals concerning the possible closure of the Wishford and Heytesbury stations and withdrawal of passenger services from Wilton North, Wylye, and Codford stations were referred to a meeting of the County Executive Committee, Wiltshire Branch, National Farmers Union at Devizes on Wednesday. It was stated the proposals were set out in a letter from British Railways and the County NFU Parliamentary Committee had received comments of the South Wilts and Warminster Branches.

After taking into account the views of the branches concerned the Executive agreed to raise no objection to the proposed closure of Wishford and Heytesbury stations. So far as withdrawal of passenger trains from Wilton North, Wylye and Codford was concerned it was also agreed to commend their acceptance, subject to the proviso that passenger train service be limited to early morning and late evening trains at Wylye station only.

The NFU's agreement to the discontinuance of freight services was subject to vehicular distribution from railheads at Salisbury and Warminster without additional charge.

Local newspapers in early September 1955 gave notice of pending closure of stations: CLOSING OF WISHFORD AND HEYTESBURY STATIONS WITHDRAWAL OF PASSENGER TRAIN SERVICE FROM WILTON NORTH, WYLYE AND CODFORD STATIONS.

On and from Monday, 19th September, 1955, Wishford and Heytesbury stations will be closed entirely and the passenger train services withdrawn from Wilton North, Wylye and Codford stations, which will remain open for parcels and freight traffic. British Railways will continue to provide collection and delivery services throughout the area for parcels and Freight traffic. Facilities for truckload traffic and small consignments at present handed in or collected at Wishford and Heytesbury will be available at adjacent stations.

Further information may be obtained from the Station Master or Goods Agent, Salisbury (Telephone Salisbury 2201): Station Masters Wilton North (Telephone Wilton3248): Wylye (Telephone Wylye 226): Codford (Telephone Codford St. Mary 204): Warminster (Telephone Warminster 2002 (passenger) or 2383 (freight)) or from District Traffic Superintendant, British Railways, Woking, Surrey (TelephoneWoking 2424).

Alternative bus facilities in the area are provided jointly by the Wilts & DorsetMotor Services Ltd. and The Western National Omnibus Co. Ltd. who operate a frequent service between Salisbury and Warminster. A service is also provided by Wylye Valley Motor Services to and from Salisbury.

Public notices were put up at all stations on the line to inform passengers of the date of closure.

The Salisbury Journal 23 September 1955
Wylye Valley Stations close down

An N Gauge model of Wishford Goods Shed built by the Author.

Despite strong complaints made by the Salisbury Branch of the National Farmers Union and many other organizations to the Chief Commercial Manager of the Southern Region of British Railways the Wishford and Heytesbury stations were closed on Monday. On the same day the passenger train services were withdrawn from Wilton North, Wylye and Codford.

The line remains operational with regular trains, Waterloo to Bristol Temple Meads via Salisbury operated by South West Trains and Portsmouth to Cardiff operated by First Great Western, however there are now no stations between Salisbury and Warminster. There are regular steam hauled excursions, starting and finishing at a vareity of locations, most taking water at Salisbury.

4387 heads the down 0812 Bristol to Southampton train on 20/7/1937 at Heytesbury.

CHAPTER 2
TRACKWORK AND PLATFORMS

Initially there was a single track of broad gauge dimensions laid with one platform at the end of which was a left hand point into the sidings, going through the goods shed, and returning to the main line via another point. This siding had a reverse point leading to an end dock short siding and a further point into the coal sidings, at the opposite end there was a head shunt which stopped before the bridge over a lane leading to Grovely Woods.

In 1874 at the time of gauge conversion to 'narrow gauge' there do not appear to be any other track alterations. Around 1898 a passing loop was put into place, a point at the Warminster end and a point which is considered to have been alongside the goods shed (no definitive data can be found on changes to trackwork

The cattle dock and associated siding.

other than a 1909 drawing which shows the horse dock siding). A 1901 OS Map shows the single track being split at the Warminster end to give the passing loop, the point the other end is rather indistinct but does appear to be alongside the goods shed. This map clearly shows that the Station Master's house has yet to be built, but the Warminster end point is approximately alongside where this was eventually built. This 1901 map also shows the second, up platform, in place and connected to the main platform via a footbridge.

Later in 1901 the track was doubled in both directions and the point at the Warminster end removed, but the point alongside the goods shed still in place. At this time it is considered that a crossover from the up line to the main sidings was put in place (crossing over the down line and into the goods shed sidings).

In 1909 the sidings for the horse dock were put in place, accessed by a point leading back into them off of the up line just to the Salisbury end of the platform. At this time the head shunt from the goods shed leading to the overbridge (Wilton end SU079352) was extended over this bridge and required the bridge to be widened to take three tracks. After 1909 there do not appear to be any further track alterations until after closure of the station.

Because the station was on a relatively tight curve there was a speed restriction of 35m.p.h. in place until the early 1970's when the trackwork was re-aligned and the speed restriction changed to 50m.p.h. and is still in force in 2012.

The underside of the bridge at Grovely Road. The line between the original bridge on the left and the new brickwork of the widened bridge of 1909. (SU087352)

The old station buildings at Heytesbury, now belonging to a private house.

Stations were built at Heytesbury, Codford, Wylye, Langford (a halt that closed very soon after the line opened to passenger traffic) Wishford and Wilton and remained open until final closure to passenger traffic on 19 September 1955 (some stations, but not Wishford, remained open for goods traffic for almost another 10 years), as this was a Monday the last train was on the preceding Saturday – 17 September 1955. Most of the main station buildings were of a similar design (this design by R P Brereton, who worked for and alongside I K Brunel and took over many of Brunel's Projects after his death). Also many of the stations on the Weymouth line were of a similar design. Additionally most of the stations that can be seen, today, on the West Somerset Railway are similar and also designed by R P Brereton, albeit built at a slightly later date than Wishford.

The stonemason for both the main station building and the goods shed was a Mr. Brimmer, his remit was 'to build from best local stone'. It is most probable the stone came from the Chilmark quarries. The stonework for the main station building being fully faced and the goods shed being more roughly faced.

Access to the main station building was through a standard GWR, wide gate and up the station approach. To the left of the approach roadway was the siding used for coal, this extended almost to the road boundary. Immediately to the left of the station building and to the rear was the short siding used for milk churns.

To the right of the main station building (viewed from the roadway) there was a wooden gate leading to the platform. It appears this gate may have been used

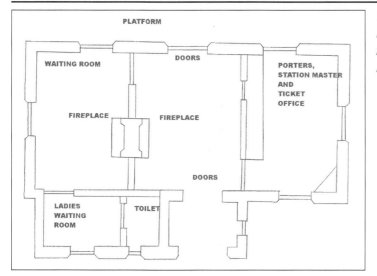

The internal layout of the main station building.

to enter the station building from the platform rather than using the double doors at the station approach side. Also on this side was the Gents toilet and a gate to the Station Master's garden. To the left of the main building, and on the platform there was another gate (for station staff use) giving access to the short siding.

The station from opening to c1898 had only one platform, of some 400 feet in length, which had a single storey building similar to numerous other country GWR stations in this area and on the line to Weymouth, this was built of local stone with a tall chimney, to one side of the centre and topped with two chimney pots, with another shorter chimney to the rear right hand side at the lower end of the roof (this being removed somewhere before the early 1930's and being replaced by a stove pipe chimney to the line side of the centre of the building and close to the wall at the Warminster end) and with a canopy over the platform door and almost the entire front of the building (in the centre of the canopy is a small stove pipe chimney to allow fumes, and heat, to escape from the oil lamp below the canopy). The building had the ticket office on one side and waiting room on the other side which led to a Ladies Waiting Room containing its own toilet. Outside, near the platform access gate, there was a gent's toilet built of brick with a slate roof and containing 3 urinal stalls and 1 w.c. (as this is brick built it is considered it was most probably built at the same time as the up platform, and the original cast iron urinal then being re-sited on the up platform). In a photograph taken just prior to closure it shows that the central stone chimney has been reduced to roof ridge height and therefore assumed that the fireplaces in the Booking Office and Waiting Room are clearly not able to be used. In a photograph taken shortly after closure it shows a stove pipe chimney at the rear (Wilton end) corner of the Ladies Waiting Room which indicates there may have been a stove installed in that corner.

Around 1898 another platform, of some 400 feet in length, was added, this being linked to the main platform by a covered footbridge (to the north of the main platform building – the Warminster end) and had a small waiting shelter, constructed of brick with sloping roof together with a gents toilet outside which contained 3 urinal stalls. This now gave a total length of platform of some 800 ft, each platform being 10 ft wide. Both platforms were lit by oil lights (of standard GWR design), 3 on the main platform building, one at each end of the footbridge, 2 on the other platform building and others along the length of each platform. At the Salisbury end of the up platform (opposite side to the main station building) was a standard GWR design lamp hut for storage of paraffin for lamps and other items that could pose a danger to the public.

Each platform had one Running in Board (GWR terminology for Station Nameboard), on the down platform sited between the overbridge and gents toilet and just behind the platform railings, the up platform one being sited between the lamp hut and waiting shelter (again behind the platform railings). Each one had support posts made of bridge rail rather than the normal wooden posts. Each

The four elevations of the original station building.

28

platform surface was blue diamond brick in front of the main buildings and compacted gravel for the rest. The edges at the rail side were flat stone of a similar colour to the stone used for the main building.

On 1 April 1895 a Contract was placed with Daniel Panter a Building Contractor of Broughton, Pershore, Worcestershire for a total sum of £1561 2s 3d. This Contract being for erection of 2 footbridges, one at Codford and one at Wishford, the building of up platforms, complete with waiting shelters, at both locations and in addition it also covered building cattle pens, extending the down platform and a water supply at Codford Station. The total sum of works at Wishford was: New Up Platform £102 10s 8d; New Waiting Shed and urinals £245 3s 3d; Footbridge £309 18s 11d.

The works at Wishford also covered erection of 11 in no. CI Platform Standards and fitting of Glazed Lanterns and for the fitting of 4 Glazed Lanterns to brackets.

It appears that the works for the footbridges cannot have been carried out by

A photo taken in 1930's with Station Master (most probably Frederick Fawden) and the other 4 staff who worked at the station. To the right there is a NE wagon on the siding and at the right hand base of the signal box is a Broad Gauge type hand operated quadrant point lever. Although not shown on the photograph there is another single window on the rear of the signal box so that the signalman can view the operation in the sidings.

this contractor as another Contract was placed on 8 November 1895 with Knight & Gregory of Trevor House, Keppoch, Roath, Cardiff for the sum of £312 18s 11d for Wishford and a similar sum for Codford. A barrow way constructed of sleepers connected the two platforms at the Salisbury end of the platforms.

Under the Railways Valuation for Rating Act 1930 the Estimated Capital Value of the station area inclusive of buildings, platforms, roadways, fences and dead sidings was £1447. A further breakdown was: Waiting room built of Brick, slate and wood with a height of 12ft – value £44; Urinal with 3 stalls; Oil store – value £3; Sawdust store – value £4; Lavatory of brick glass and slate – value £39 (4 stalls inc 1 WC); Footbridge of steel – value £400; Platforms 800ft x 10ft – value £316; Branchlines 323 ft – value £162; Goods shed – value £561; Approach – value £25; Cattle pen – value £10; Loading way – value £83; Weighbridge and hut – value £5 (let to G M Young); Coal wharf 80ft x 10ft and 40ft x 10ft (let to G M Young) 180 sq yards; And 80 sq yards let to E Carey; Poultry runs let to E C West; Station building Height 13ft 6 ins, flat roof 13ft, parcels office and cloakroom 8ft 6ins; Goods shed height 24ft with lean to office and canopy. Platforms 11ft 6ins x 13ft, 9ft 6ins x 45ft 6ins, 9ft 6ins x 13ft 3ins.

On 6 December 1946 a Contract was placed with Wort & Way of 37 Castle Street, Salisbury for the sum of £244 2s 9d for the provision of a septic tank along with all the associated building and plumbing works.

This contract was not started by Wort & Way, who gave an explanation that they were unable to obtain men from the Labour Exchange and did not feel justified to stop work on housing for this job. The Contract was therefore cancelled by the Great Western Railway on 27 February 1948.

It does however appear a septic tank was put in place at a later date, the location of which is currently unknown. Mains Sewerage to Great Wishford was not fully installed until c1964 and as such it is anticipated this septic tank would most probably have been in the garden of the Station Master's House and served both Station building and House.

In September 1950 boundary changes took place and Wishford now came under BR(SR). The station was not re-painted in SR Green and little else was done other than to change signal posts from GWR square posts to SR lattice posts.

Although in the years after 1951 stations had 'totems', no evidence can be found of Wishford ever having totems – possibly because it was clear at that time this station was destined for closure. In 1953 when Chris Joseph moved into the Station House, with his parents, his father working on the railway at Salisbury,

Diesel Railcar No1. On the 1410 service from Salisbury to Bristol on 15/9/1936 at Stockton Dairy Farm Bridge (ST973385). This is the only known photo of a diesel railcar on the line, this service stopped in 1939. The 'fog man's hut' was replaced in the 1950s by a concrete one and remains there today.

they had to pump water from a well to the house and so it is assumed the same is true for the station. In 1946 Messrs Guthrie Allsebrook were awarded a Contract from the GWR Deeds Dept. at Paddington Station for the sum of £165 0s 0d to:

Supply 3 man and tackle and sink a borehole 35 ft. deep through the bottom of the existing 50 ft. deep well, lining the upper part with 6 ½ ins. outside dia. and ¼ ins. thick coated steel tube (20 ft. of tube provided) together with shoe, guide hopper (for top) pudlog and clip (for building into well to fix top tube). Extend suction of the existing hand pump to draw from the boring.

Over the period from 19 September 1955 (date of closure) to 1983 the site was run down and buildings and trackwork were progressively removed but the signal box remained operational until 1964. The Station Master's house was sold in 1976 and the last remaining building, the goods shed, was demolished in 1983. Up until closure the Station Clock was a 14 inch dial wooden cased Single Fusee

Dropcase Clock with a number of 2147W and reported as having a replaced and re-lettered dial with the manufacturer noted as John Walker & Sons, South Molton St., London. After closure the clock was transferred to the Salisbury Yard Foremans Cabin, West End, and later to Salisbury Starting Cabin. This clock came up for auction on 12/9/2009 under Lot 199, Sheffield Railwayanna, but was not sold as it did not reach its reserve price.

Sheffield Railwayanna Catalogue details:

BR(S) 14" DIAL WOODEN CASED SINGLE FUSEE DROPCASE CLOCK with a replaced and re-lettered dial "John Walker & Sons South Molton Street London" and the number "2147W". The "W" suffix indicates a clock that was transferred into the region following boundary changes etc. According to the official records, 2147W was originally allocated to Wishford Platform (ex-GWR then Western Region), then it was transferred to Salisbury Yard Foreman's Cabin (West End) and finally to Salisbury Shunting Cabin. The back case is 25" long and 10" wide. We understand the clock is in full working order and is complete with wooden pendulum with adjustable cast iron weight and winder.

For a number of years around 1980 this clock was in the Royal Oak public house in Great Wishford.

8327 hauls a rake of LSWR and SR coaches on the 1635 Cardiff to Portsmouth train on 19/7/1937 and taken on the approaches to Heytesbury station.

CHAPTER 3
THE SIGNAL BOX AND TIMETABLES

Between the goods shed and the main station building, and on the end of the down platform, was a signal box, erected in 1895, built of brick and wood and to the same standard pattern of many others of the period. This replaces an earlier box erected April 1887. The signal box remained in use until 26 August 1964 and it was removed soon after.

Little is known about the 1887 signal box but as it was built at the same time as Heytesbury and Wylye then it is considered it 'may' have been to a similar design, this presumably would have been built about the time of change from the use of 'constables'. The Signal Box Register reports the signal box as of GWR Design and 25ft 1ins by 12ft with 23 levers set at 5 ¼ inch centres and using a relatively standard GWR type locking frame.

Communication with other stations was initially by Single Needle Telegraph, this still being in place in 1873 (the 1873 Service Timetable notes: This line worked by Single Needle Telegraph). If, and when later forms of telegraph were fitted is not known, neither is it known when telephones were installed.

In 1909, when the cattle dock siding was laid, the signal box had 20 levers in use and 3 spares. A later signal box diagram of 1945 shows only 2 spares, levers 17 and 18. Because the station is on a sharp curve the track is super elevated through the platforms with the high rail towards the down platform.

In the latter years the signalman only worked from 7.30 am to 7.15 pm excluding Sundays when the signal box was shut. This signal box and some others on the line were switched out allowing all signals to be cleared to a 'proceed' aspect on Sundays when there was no signal man present. Trains could, if necessary stop at the station but not use the sidings, or crossover between up and down lines. (Wilton North and Wylye signal boxes were open on Sundays).

For most of the lines life the signals were GWR lower quadrant signals on square wooden posts. Later photographs show signals are of a Southern type of upper quadrant on a steel lattice post. Although no evidence can be found as to

33

SIGNAL & POINT LEVERS

1 Up Distant signal – 804 yards from signal box
2 Up Home signal – 96 yards from signal box
3 Up Starting signal – 253 yards from signal box
4 Ground signal for exit of horse dock siding
5 Point on up line leading to horse dock siding
6 Ground signal for entry into horse dock
7 Ground signal on down line crossover to up line
8 Crossover points Up Line to Down Line
9 Ground signal on up line crossover to down line
10 Ground signal on down line, for entry back into good shed siding
11 Points down line into goods shed siding and headshunt
12 Ground signal goods shed siding headshunt point
13 Ground signal from goods shed siding to crossover and up line
14 Crossover points Goods Shed road to Up Line
15 Ground signal for crossover from up line into goods shed siding
16 Lever to operate Up Line detonator placer
17 Spare
18 Spare
19 Lever to operate Down Line detonator placer
20 Down advanced Starting signal – 400 yards from signal box
21 Down Starting signal – 19 yards from signal box
22 Down Home signal – 151 yards from signal box
23 Down Distant signal – 1267 yards from signal box
No 21 is locked by Track A, No 2 is locked by Track B.
Tracks lock starting signals in rear boxes and control block.
Distant signals interlocked with block.

when these were changed it is probable it was during 1950 when the station was transferred to Southern Region from Western Region, certainly the line from Castle Carey to Weymouth were changed during this year.The signal box had a bracket on the front and this was used by the Ordnance Survey as a trigonometry point and had a reference as SU 079 352.

Special Instructions for Wishford were:

Reg 13 (a) A train or vehicle provided there is a brake van at the rear with a man in it and the B.B.S. outside Home Signal has been sent and acknowledged by the signalman at the rear.

It is understood this deals with setting vehicles back on a falling gradient, outside the home signal, towards the signal box in the rear. This required a braked vehicle at the rear in case any vehicles ran away in the wrong direction, such as when a coupling broke during a shunting movement with vehicles not fitted with continuous brake. A bell signal would be sent to the signal box in the rear to protect the movement and prevent acceptance of another train.)"

Reg 24 (c) It will not be necessary to place the signals at danger for a train which calls at Wishford during the time this signal box is switched out unless the train remains stationary an unusually long time.

In order to guard against a runaway whenever a vehicle has to be detached from an up train at the platform the Signalman must as soon as a train comes to a stand and the last vehicle is clear of the trailing points turn those points for the loading dock and they must remain in that position until the vehicle has been cleared of the Up Line. Special attention is directed to the prohibition contained in No 3 Appendix to the Service T.T on the placing of passenger coaching stock in the Cattle Dock Siding.

Prior to the first known signal box being erected the signaling and point operation would have been carried out by a 'constable' who may have had a small hut similar to a sentry box. No information has been found on signaling and point operation in the early days of the station. A 1930's photograph shows a Broad Gauge type point lever, for operation of the point between the end loading dock and the coal siding, and situated at the Salisbury end of the signal box.

During the first 30 years of operation there were 4 trains in each direction on weekdays and 1 on Sundays. This Sunday service was to oblige Parliamentary requirements of every station having at least one service per day. The 1865 timetable shows:

Salisbury (depart 08.05) stopping at all stations to Bristol (arriving 10.35) – stopping Wishford at 08.20.

Bristol (depart 17.30) stopping all stations to Salisbury (arriving 20.35) – stopping Wishford at 20.17.

Albeit the line had not formally been opened to passenger traffic yet, the Salisbury Journal of 28 June 1856 denoted a Great Western Railway Timetable for Warminster to Salisbury with the following times:

Salisbury to Warminster:

Salisbury 6.40 10.05 1.00 5.10

Warminster to Salisbury

Warminster 10.05 1.00 3.00 8.15

The Salisbury and Winchester Journal of 5 July 1856 and 12 July 1856 showed the same times.

Trains stopping at Wishford from Westbury to Salisbury

Year

1872 6.55 10.36 1.54 6.55

1902 8.20 10.15 12.04 3.30 4.33 6.05 8.21

1920 8.18 10.25 12.31 3.06 5.40 8.32

1947 7.20 9.25 12.00 5.43 8.50

Trains stopping at Wishford from Salisbury to Westbury

Year

1902 5.50 7.50 9.10 10.30 1.05 2.35 4.55 7.35 8.10

1920 7.35 9.34 12.58 2.55 4.56 7.56

1947 7.25 9.35 12.50 4.52 7.35

The journey from Wishford to Salisbury had timings as short as 10 minutes but the most common duration was 15 minutes. The travel time from Wishford to Westbury was generally 45 minutes.

On Sundays, in later years, there were no trains in either direction stopping at Wishford.

Throughout the period Wishford was open there was a pick up/drop off freight service twice a day, one up, and one down between Salisbury and Westbury. This

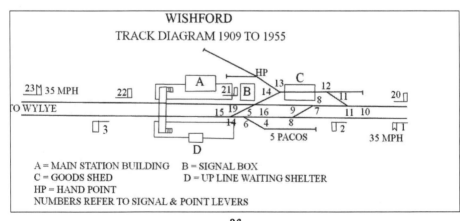

WISHFORD
TRACK DIAGRAM 1909 TO 1955

A = MAIN STATION BUILDING   B = SIGNAL BOX
C = GOODS SHED   D = UP LINE WAITING SHELTER
HP = HAND POINT
NUMBERS REFER TO SIGNAL & POINT LEVERS

service was shared between Salisbury and Westbury crews, with a crew change usually at Heytesbury.

Although the timetables for stopping trains appears to give the appearance of a very quiet country line, perhaps the opposite is true as there was much freight traffic and numerous through, no stopping passenger trains.

The Summer 1951 Weekday Service Timetable shows 1 freight and 6 passenger trains stopping at Wishford plus 13 freight and 5 non stopping trains on the Up Line (Saturdays there are a further 3 freight and 6 passenger trains, all non stopping). The down line shows 2 freight and 5 passenger stopping with 8 freight and 4 passenger non stopping (Saturdays an additional 5 non stopping passenger trains). Locomotives being from 28xx, 43xx, 72xx, Grange, Hall, Star and Castle Classes.

From line opening to 1896 trains only ran between Bristol and Salisbury, requiring a change for other locations. From 1896 through trains ran between Cardiff and Portsmouth, and in later years there were trains to Bournemouth and Brighton.

Coal trains from locations in South Wales, initially terminating at Salisbury ran though day and night, some changing locos at Salisbury to go onwards to Portsmouth and Southampton.

Over the period 1908 to 1933 the traffic dealt with at Wishford is as follows:

Year	No. Staff	Tickets issued	Season Tickets	Goods (tons)	Livestock (Wagons)	Total Receipts	Staff Wages
1908	5	12340	No info	2256	28	£3,600	£302
1913	4	10943	No info	2289	86	£3,140	£270
1923	5	8102	55	3976	95	£5,170	£771
1924	5	7654	62	3683	101	£4,774	£780
1925	5	7802	44	5273	105	£6,463	£791
1926	5	6654	30	4433	127	£5,474	£737
1927	5	7513	29	4422	125	£5,273	£790
1928	5	6863	23	4641	115	£5,471	£777
1929	5	6647	21	4024	75	£5,082	£716
1930	5	5942	19	2850	78	£3,883	£755
1931	5	4906	24	2155	81	£3,081	£719
1932	5	4740	31	2287	74	£3,027	£704
1933	5	3994	34	2022	70	£2,452	£693

CHAPTER 4
TRAINS

The line was originally built as a single track Broad Gauge (7 foot 0 ¼ inches) on longtitudinal sleepers.

Observations of Broad Gauge trains:
Sun Class 2-2-2 (6ft driving wheels):
Sunbeam – observed on opening day of the branch
Javelin – observed on opening day of the branch
Leo Class 2-4-0 (5ft driving wheels):
Virgo - involved in accident at Salisbury Station on 6 October 1856
Fury Class 2-6-0 (5ft driving wheels):
Bergion – involved in accident at Salisbury Station 6 October 1856
Bogie Class 4-4-0ST (5ft 9ins driving wheels):
Homer – involved in accident at Skew Bridge Salisbury 5/8/1873
Caesar Class 0-6-0 (5ft driving wheels):
Gladiator – involved in accident at Skew Bridge Salisbury 5/8/1873
Nemesis
Victoria Class 2-4-0 tender engine (6ft 6ins. driving wheels):
Napoleon, Oscar, Abdul Medjid
Firefly class 2-2-2 (7ft driving wheels):
Mentor, Arrow, Comet
Hercules class 0-6-0 (5ft coupled driving wheels)
Tityos
Caliph goods class 0-6-0 (5 ft coupled driving wheels)
Nemesis
Waverley class 4-4-0 (7ft driving wheels)
Ivanhoe, Rob Roy, Coeur de Lion, Lalla Rookh
Metropolitan Class – 2-4-0 (6ft driving wheels) – converted to tender engines
Hornet, Lily, Myrtle, Laurel -– all based at Salisbury c1864 to c1873

38

Ex Vale of Neath 0-6-0 ST converted 0-6-0 tender engines, No 13, No 14, No 15

For a few years prior to gauge conversion there were daily coal trains from Bullo Pill Pit in the Forest of Dean. Because the Severn Tunnel had yet to be built these trains were routed via Gloucester, Swindon and Chippenham to Salisbury.

Prior to full passenger and goods carrying traffic after gauge conversion the first train was from Bristol to Salisbury (with a Salisbury driver Mr Roffey accompanied by a Salisbury based fireman) with empty passenger stock and left Bristol soon after midday, one further train of passenger empties soon followed as did a goods train of empties.

The first standard gauge train from Bristol to Salisbury had Dean 2-4-0 Metro Tank No. 615 at its head. It appears 514 was used for goods traffic on this line during 1916.

From their introduction in 1928 the Hall class were the most prominent locomotive on passenger traffic that stopped at all stations, usually with 5 non-corridor coaches of the surburban type, many photos show 4 toplights and a clerestory (from the 1930's corridor stock was usually used, and in particular on Cardiff to Portsmouth trains).

GWR railcars were used on occasion. One such occasion is captured (on photograph) by H C Casserley in September 1936 where the railcar is on the Westbury Salisbury and return on 14.10 Salisbury to Westbury. From 1934 to 1939 there was one service per day, weekdays only.

Observations of Standard Gauge trains

517 class 0-4-0T: 552, 848, 1481

Armstrong Goods 0-6-0: 789 allocated to Salisbury 1921

1076 class 0-6-0: 1619 allocated to Salisbury 1921

1701 class 0-6-0ST: 1704 allocated to Salisbury 1921

Dean Goods 0-6-0: 2047, 2357 allocated Salisbury 1934, 2301, 2415,2433, 2565 allocated to Salisbury 1921, 2375, 2407 on 10.25 Cardiff Salisbury on 5/5/19502412 based Salisbury during 1938

Aberdare class 2-6-0 tender engine: 2601, 2617 allocated to Salisbury 1921, 2618 ,2640 ,26352671 allocated to Salisbury 1921 Used on both passenger and goods trains.

28xx class 2-8-0 tender engine: 2815 regular on freight, 2820, 2836, 2870 allocated to Salisbury 1934; 2857 new to Salisbury 1918, 2812, 2814 allocated to Salisbury 1938; 2833, 2844, 2877 allocated to Salisbury 1921, 2886, 2893,

3864. Used on both coal and general goods trains.

Barnum Class 2-4-0: 3208 on Bristol Portsmouth passenger with LSWR coaches; 3221 Westbury based 24/10/1924 with Portsmouth passenger of 3rd clerestory, arch roof passenger brake, lav composite clerestory, 3rd clerestory, 3rd clerestory, 3rd clerestory, passenger brake. 3217 allocated to Salisbury 1921

Bulldog Class 4-4-0: 3306 Amorel allocated to Salisbury 1934; 3308 Falmouth

Duke Class 4-4-0: 3313 Cotswold, 3316Guernsey, 3317 Jersey allocated to Salisbury 1901

Bulldog Class 4-4-0: 3321 Brasenose; 3329 Mars, at Salisbury during 1929; 3334 Tavy, 3361 Edward VI; 3391 Dominion of Canada allocated to Salisbury 1934; 3364 Frank Bibby, on 3.43 Bradford on Avon Salisbury passenger on 8 July 1938. 3376 River Plym, 3401 Vancouver; 3431 loco not named, allocated to Salisbury 1934

Atabra Class 4-4-0: 3410 (Cardiff based) on 14.27 Bristol Salisbury with 4 coaches on 6/3/1911; 3411 Stanley Baldwin on Bath to Salisbury passenger 2/9/1916 In collision with 2557 at Warminster on this date.

Bird Class 4-4-0: 3443 Chaffinch allocated to Salisbury 1921; 3446 Goldfinch allocated to Salisbury 1938

Star Class 4-6-0: 4045 Prince John on Cardiff to Portsmouth passenger with 6 SR coaches (set number 436) in 1938. 4015 Knight of St. John, 4020 Knight Commander, 4028 Romanian Monarch, 4033 Queen Victoria, 4050 Princess Alice, 4055 Princess Sophia, 4069 Margam Abbey

Badminton class 4-4-0: 4103 Besborough,

Flower class 4-4-0 4115 Marigold, 4156 Gardenia, 4165 Narcissus

Atabra class 4-4-0: 4127 Ladysmith, 4137 Wolseley, 4146 Sydney,

Armstrong Class 0-6-0 4172 Gooch

Saint Class 4-6-0: 2928 Saint Sebastian, 2931 Arlington Court

42xx, 52xx, 72xx 2-8-0T: 4206, 4226, 4259, 4266, 4286 ; 5220, 5242; 7202 regular on Radyr to Salisbury coal trains; 7205, 7207, 7209

43xx – 2-6-0 tender engine: 4332, 4339, 4354, 4368, 4380; 5306, 5307, 5325; 6303, 6316, 6328, 6355, 6368, 6375, 6387; 7307 allocated to Salisbury 1934, 7309; 8300, 8328, 8352, 8329 allocated to Salisbury 1934; 4575 Prairie 2-6-2T; 4595, 5548, 5549

47xx 2-8-0: 4702 on Westbury to Salisbury coal trains in 1942; N.B. This class of loco was both before, and after WWII not allowed on this line due to its overall weight and its axle loading.

Castle class 4-6-0: 4084 Aberystwyth Castle, 4094 Dynever Castle, 5005 Manorbier Castle, 5062 Earl of Shaftesbury, 5090 Neath Abbey, 5096 Bridgewater Castle 5080 Defiant and 4968 Shotton Hall double headed on last passenger train 5.02 Salisbury Cardiff on 17/9/1955

Hall class 4-6-0: 5902 Howick Hall, 5904 Kelham Hall, 5913 Rushton Hall, 5925 Eastcote Hall, 6909 Frewin Hall, 6935 Browsholme Hall, 6939 Calveley Hall, 6966 Witchimingham Hall, 6979 Helperley Hall, 4944 Middleton Hall, 6978 Haroldstone Hall – allocated Salisbury 1947; 3950 Garth Hall (as an oil burner) on Portsmouth Cardiff passenger on 13/3/1948

56xx – 0-6-2 tank: 6618, 6699; Used on coal trains as train loco and as banker.

Grange class 4-6-0: 6804 Brockington Grange, 6818 Hardwick Grange, 6833 Calcot Grange, 6836 Estevarney Grange, 6845 Paviland Grange, 6850 Cleeve Grange, 6868 Penros Grange, 6876 Kingsland Grange, 6870 Bodicote Grange, 6846 Ruckley Grange new to Salisbury 1938; 6876 Kingsland Grange

Manor class 4-6-0: 7804 Baydon Manor, 7809 Childrey Manor

King Class 4-6-0: GWR King class were not allowed on the line due to weight restrictions, however, there is one report that one of this class did haul a passenger train from Westbury to Salisbury, as apparently this was the only loco in steam and immediately available to replace a failed loco at Westbury. This is an unconfirmed report where date/year and loco number are unknown.

WD class 2-8-0: 79226

8F class 2-8-0: 8443, 8454, 8470, 8456, 8436, 8432, 8414, 8440 Usually seen on coal trains from South Wales to Salisbury.

SR U Class 2-6-0: 1625, 1624 Both of these locos based at Salisbury for a number of years.

LNER B12's (4-6-0) on Ambulance trains from Portsmouth and Southampton to USA base at Musgrove Park near Taunton during WWII. 8509, 8516, 8519, 8547, 8555 & 8557.

Please note that this is not a definitive listing of all locomotives that ran on the line, it is merely a listing of those found in a variance of references and photographs, however it does give a 'flavour' of the variance of locomotives that were used on the line.

During the period 1908 to 1911 there was a service run by Steam Railmotor, starting either at Cardiff or Bristol on a Sunday evening and reaching Salisbury at 21.00 where it was stabled overnight and returned 05.55 on Monday morning. The purpose of this very early morning train must have been for parcels, perishables and milk as it always ran pulling a 'siphon'.

In later years the first train on a Monday could easily be the normal 5 coaches and as many as 11 brown vehicles (milk, parcels, perishables etc.)

In 1934 the GWR General Manager asked for an additional 13 diesel railcars, one of which was for a service to Salisbury. This service ran weekdays only running Bristol, reaching Westbury 13.12, Warminster 13.20 and Salisbury 13.45 and not stopping at intermediate stations. It returned from Salisbury at 14.10 stopping at all stations, Wishford 14.22. This service was terminated in September 1939 and did not start again after WWII.

Passenger trains brought in daily and weekly papers (usually down line at about 0800), some of these were collected by Mr. Carter on his bicycle and he delivered them to Jack Bundy who ran the newspaper business in Shrewton. Mail was also delivered to the station, by 1904 the postbag from Devizes was picked up every day by Mr. Brands by pony and trap, another was picked up by Mr. Phillimore on his tricycle, both of these for Shrewton.

Wishford had a fishmonger, Bert Hiscocks, who traveled by train to Wilton to pick up fish which he delivered round the village.

In the late 1920's and early 1930's the children from Wishford (and other villages on the line) who had passed the exam for the Grammar School traveled on the 8.08 to Salisbury to go to Bishops School or the Grammar School near Victoria Park, often a train with as many as 8 non-corridor coaches, where the girls and boys traveled generally in separate compartments. because the return train was up to 20 minutes before 5.00 pm from Salisbury this meant they had to leave school early.

During the 1930's most local freight came from Westbury, loaded wagons being detached from the 07.15 from Westbury which dropped wagons at all stations to Salisbury. Through freight, mainly long coal trains (of up to 56 wagons) came from South Wales, to Salisbury and/or Portsmouth. the mid morning Bristol to Salisbury freight train regularly dropped off the odd coal wagon at many of the stations, this train was usually pulled by a Dean Goods loco. loaded wagons were picked up by the early evening Salisbury to Westbury goods, leaving empties to be picked up by the early morning goods from Salisbury, sometimes being worked by 3306 Bulldog Class, arriving before the first passenger train. At times in WWII some trains ran late but they always ran.

During the 50's (and many of the earlier years) most of the trains were at least 5 coaches (corridor stock) but more commonly 6, and sometimes additionally at least one siphon (a GWR brown vehicle with slatted sides to keep milk and other consumables cool or for parcels and post) which could be Western Region (ex-GWR) stock or Southern stock and sometimes a combination of both, normally pulled by Halls or Granges but it was not unusual to see a Southern loco (usually an S15 or U class) at its head. These trains were either Bristol or Cardiff to Portsmouth Harbour. There was also a service from Brighton to Cardiff that ran alternate days with GWR and SR stock, the SR stock appears to be set 436 comprising of 4 or 5 coaches from 3rd Corridor Brake 3188, 1st Corridor 7186, 3rd Corridor 1204, 3rd Corridor 722, 3rd Corridor 721 and 3rd Corridor Brake 3189 (all coaches are 'Ironclad'), the corresponding GWR set was set 223 comprising of Van 3rd, 3 composite, 3rd and a van 3rd. SR Sets 866, 867 and 873 also appear to have run between Brighton and Cardiff. GWR stock has been reported as M Set of Third Brake, Third, Composite, Brake Third (all Corridor stock). From about 1940 passenger sets have been reported as K Set comprising of Brake Third, Third, Composite, Composite, Brake Third (all Corridor stock).

The 10.30 Cardiff to Portsmouth, and the 09.33 Portsmouth to Cardiff ran with two extra 3rd coaches. The 1635 Cardiff to Portsmouth ran with an extra 3rd at the rear. The 0810 Bristol to Portsmouth ran with a Siphon G, next to the engine, for parcels and post.

The 0725 Salisbury to Bristol had a Siphon for empty milk churns for Melksham (dropped at Westbury).

The last train, on 17 September 1955 (line formally closed 19 September but as no stopping passenger trains on Sundays the last passenger ran on 17 September), from Salisbury to Cardiff, was the 5.02 headed by 5080 Defiant (now preserved at Tysley Birmingham Steam Museum) and 4968 Shotton Hall. This occasion went without fuss or special occasion. One of the last trains from Bristol to Salisbury was the 4.32 headed by 5904 Kelham Hall with a train of 1 goods vehicle and 5 coaches.

The line still has many steam hauled trains every year from a variance of starting and end locations. VSOE (Venice Simplon Orient Express) has been seen, sometimes steam hauled. In latter years steam haulage has been by many classes of loco, but most would never have worked the line in steam days. During 2010 to 2012 locos seen were 34067, 44932, 60019, 60163, 70000, 70013 and 71000.

CHAPTER 5
STATION MASTER'S HOUSE & STAFF

It is unclear as to when the Station Master's house was built, it is not shown on either the 1879 or 1901 maps of the station area. It is considered it must have been built c1902 from its design which is similar to others built by the GWR at this time and it appears the GWR built many other staff residences during this period. When it was built it had a garden some 300 feet long

Station Master's house (now called Station House) taken 2012. The extension at the right hand side was built in 1990/91 and is complementary to the main building even down to the blue bricks at the base of the house. At the entrance is a 'replica' totem that may have been seen if the station had remained open and in BR(WR) control.

The station end of the garden ran parallel to the station approach, angled back from the road and with a gate, close to the railway line boundary, for the stationmaster. There was a path from this gate alongside the railway boundary up to the house. Within the garden was a well that supplied water for the house and the station, the water being hand pumped to both locations. During WWII there was a shelter in the garden for 'family' use (only two other houses in the village had their own shelters).

Chris Joseph and his family, Father Thomas – who worked at Salisbury Station, Mother Eifron and Brother Jonathan, moved into the Station House in 1953 and lived there until 1976. Chris can remember watching the Coronation on their television soon after moving in. The house was sold by British Rail in 1976. The house remains today, albeit extended in 1990/91, as a private residence. The garden has been halved and a bungalow Green Haven has been built at the former station end of the garden.

At small stations such as Wishford, what we now know as a Station Master, was called 'Booking Constable', (sometimes also noted as Booking Porter), his uniform was much like a police constable but with an open collar. What we now know as a 'Signalman', or Signalman Porter' was then a 'Switchman' and he also wore a uniform much like a policeman with a regulation police collar. Uniforms changed quite a lot up to about 1902, Great Western Way (published by HRMS) give more definitive detail.

In PRO RAIL 264/414 is reported one of the very earliest staff at Wishford, a William Boulter who was a Booking Porter, and shown as being at Wishford from 1853 and he was aged 20 on entering service, he moved to Shrewsbury in September 1865. This is rather interesting as the Station did not start operating until June 1856! The same document reports a John Still as a Booking Porter starting at Wishford on May 30 1868, when terminology for staff changed he then became 'Station Master'. Also reported is James Isaacs a Booking Constable who was at Wishford from October 1865 to October 1867 when he moved to Wilton and resigned in Aug 1873. Another of the staff reported is William Wynne, a Booking Porter who was at Wishford from May 1868 to May 1868 when he moved to Yetminster.

Station Masters

William Boulter June 1853? – 1865 Moved to Shrewsbury. Pay 25 shillings. 1861 census gives him as Railway Station Master aged 27, born Tewkesbury, and lived with his wife Ann, at Lotmore, Great Wishford, and children William Thomas (b 1857 Bristol), Frederick (b1858 Bristol), Agnes (b1861 Wishford) 1871 census he is living at Church Stretton, with wife Ann, Agnes (b 1861 Wishford), Sarah? (b 1862 Wishford), Laura (b1866 Wishford), Harry (b 1867 Worcester). 1891 census he is Station Master at Rushbury

James Isaacs 10/1865 – 10/1867 Moved to Wilton as Station Master and resigned from service in 1873.

William Wynne 5/1868 – 5/1868 Moved to Yetminster

John Still 5/1868 – c1887. b 1822 St Giles, Middlesex. 1881 census give him as Station Master, Shop Street, Great Wishford with Harry (b1879 Wishford), and 1891 census as Retired Station Master, still resident in Great Wishford, with Rose (b 1874 Wishford), Clifford (b1879 Wishford).

James Richings c1896 – c1931 (GWR staff No 11755) came from West Cranmore. Born c1865 Wylye and 1901 census gives him as Station Master,

Wilfred Talbot, the last Station Master outside the Station Master's House.

46

Wishford (address not specific) with wife Ann, Dorothy (b 1896 Wishford), Constance (b 1897 Wishford), Margaret (b 1899 Wishford), Isabel (b 1901 Wishford). His father, b1826 appears on 1871 census as Station Master at Wylye. The 1891 census gives him as a Signalman at West Cranmore. 1911 census he is living at Railway Station House, Great Wishford and by now there are further children – William b 1902 Wishford, Kathleen b 1906 Wishford and Godfrey b 1908 Wishford. During the 1920's he was a Grade 4 Station Master earning 37 shillings 6 pence per month. Earning 29 shillings in 1900 and 37 shillings in 1903.

Frederick Thomas Fawden c1931 – c1935. Born 1892 and in 1911 he was a Booking Clerk living with his family at Knowle, Bristol. At this time his father, Arthur Fawden was a Railway District Traffic Inspector and his 17 year old sister, Ellen was a Railway Telegraphic Clerk.

Arthur Mountstevens c1935 – 2/1947 came from Grimstones. In 1911 he was a Signalman living at Upper Worle, near Weston Super Mare. Died in service aged 63 and is buried in Wishford Cemetery (not churchyard), his wife continued to live in the Station House until 1953.

Wilfred Talbot 2/1947 ?– 9/1955? when station closed.

Edmund West, a porter at the station outside the Lamp Hut with a loco crew fireman.

Derek Gane with his father, Jack Gane (a Porter) taken c1934 on the main platform.

Porters and Signalmen

P Boulter Porter (GWR staff No 24921) 1898 – 11/1899 moved to Salisbury (b 1874 Holt)

E Gunning Signalman/Porter (GWR staff No 18161) from Wilton 1899 – 5/1900 moved to Cranmore. The 1891 census has him at Barton Regis, and from birth information of his children it appears he was living at Wishford between 1886 and 1889. 1881 census gives him as ~Porter at Melcombe Regis.

W H Budden Signalman (GWR staff No 9784) 1899 – 12/1902 moved to Wylye

J Count Porter (GWR staff No 25289) from Box 11/1899 – 2/1900 moved to Corsham

J H Fowler Signalman/Porter 7/1899 – 4/1902 Absconded and resumed at Frome

A H Miles Signalman ? (GWR staff No 20411) – 4/1900 Absconded

J Edwards Porter 2/1900 – 8/1900 moved to Wylye

E J Neyen Signalman/Porter from Yatton 3/1900 – 4/1902 moved to Cranmore

E Rogers Signalman/Porter from Nailsea 8/1900 – 12/1900 moved to Clevedon

A Plant Signalman from Cranmore 5/1900 – 9/1900 moved to Yatton

Herbert Summers Signalman from Westbury 12/1900 - ???

Mr Hale Signalman/Porter from Chippenham 4/1902 – 5/1903 moved to Chippenham

Mr Scobie Signalman/Porter from Wylye 4/1902 – 1/1903 moved to Trowbridge

Mr Lathey Signalman/Porter from Yeovil Goods 1/1903 – 12/1903 moved to Grimstones

Mr Cannings Signalman/Porter from Salisbury 12/1903 - ?????

H J Witt Signalman/Porter 5/1903 – 12/1903 moved to Salisbury

William Cossens Signalman/Porter from Grimstones 8/1904 – 1/1905 moved to Pilning, born 1871 at Weymouth

W H Bonds Signalman/Porter from Brinkworth 1/1905 - ??? 1911 census at Chipping Sodbury.

Edmund Charles West Porter c1930 – 1936/37 moved to Salisbury as District Lamp Man responsible for lamps between Salisbury and Warminster and then to Westbury Goods Yard.

Born 1905 at Chippenham. In 1911 living with his family in Salisbury where his father, William Charles West (who was born in Great Wishford in 1879) was a Railway Guard.

George Bryant

Thomas Collier

George Edmonds

William E Fleming Signalman ????? - ?9/1955?

John James Gane Porter (called Jack) c1930 - ?9/1955?

Harry Jordan

Robert Parkin

Ernie Polden Ganger/Platelayer ????? - ?9/1955?

Reg C Samways Signalman/Porter born 1900 Great Wishford

Jack Vince Signalman/Porter ???? - ?9/1955?

Richard White

Reg White

John Winsborough

Miss Brenda White Signal person/office clerk 1940 – 1945

Miss White (now Mrs. Gray) was required during the war to join one of the forces, or as a land girl, or another form of work to allow men to join the forces. A vacancy came up at Wishford for a signalman and an office clerk and so she applied, and was accepted. She worked shifts 0730 to 1400 or 1400 to 1930, mainly in the signal box but also in the ticket office as a clerk. She enjoyed the work even though continual pulling signal levers being demanding for a young lady. During her time there she vividly remembers the large amount of ambulance trains on the up line and in the latter war years many troop trains on the down line, these not necessarily being on a circular or timetable but merely signaled through from Wylye as a passenger train. As Mrs Gray is the only living person I can find that worked at the station it has been rewarding that she could confirm many facts that others had told me but had not been confirmed by a second source.

Staff at the station appear to have been very helpful to passengers, one schoolboy who lived in West Street and went away to boarding school was usually helped home by a porter who would put all of his trunks and bags on a trolley and wheel it to his house. This appears to have happened each time he came home from school at the end of the term.

Other staff
Frederick Wooton – Platelayer – 1871 census
George West – Worker – 1871 census
Charles Trehorne – Railway falter – 1871 census
George Read – Platelayer – 1871 census
Richard Simper – Labourer – 1871 census
John Pile – Labourer – 1901 census

Many of the staff lived in the village, some of the latter day staff lived in the Houses at the junction of South Street and Station Road. (Jack Gane at No 1 Station Road and later 2 Oak View, Jack Vince at No 1 Oak View and Bill Fleming at 3 Oak View).

In addition to the main station staff there were others who worked in the goods yard, one of whom was Arthur Scott who worked in the wooden weigh bridge hut (which he adorned with cigarette cards) and was responsible for weighing all coal and minerals coming in and for booking in and out items (as the carriers had to pay the GWR for weight of items transported).

CHAPTER 6
SIDINGS AND FREIGHT

In the early years Wishford did have some sidings and area for goods freight (to the south and east of the down line platform) this was enhanced with new sidings in 1909 (to the south of the new up line platform), and included a cattle pen and horse loading dock, it appears (but yet to be proven) that the siding from the goods shed to the bridge over the lane up to Hadden Hill (and access to the cattle dock sidings) was extended at this time and the over bridge widened to

7231 light engine on 9/7/1938. These locos were regulars on coal trains from South Wales and unusual to see this class of loco without wagons.

51

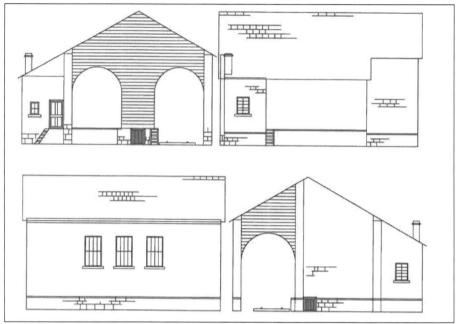

take a third track. Although drawings and specifications cannot be found it is clear that they were inspected and cleared for use on 1 September 1909. At this time the total length of the sidings was 323 yards.

Access to the goods shed and coal staithes was via set of standard GWR wide gates – up and to the left for the goods shed and up and to the right for the coal staithes, weighbridge and associated huts. The site of this gateway now forms the gateways to Weathertop and The Sidings.

The design of the goods shed was much similar to many others on both this branch and the Weymouth branch, built of 'best local stone' and clad at the ends with wood planking. On one side the siding goes right through the building, with semicircular arched entrance and exit and a platform for off loading goods, (a very poor photo taken after closure of the station shows the platform being built of stone and going from end to end of the building without a break). Pedestrian access to the top of the platform being by steps at each end. Inside and at the southern end was a further platform, pedestrian access was via the steps on the south eastern side and also providing access to the Office. The Office was built on the south eastern corner of the building and the roof taking the same slope as the main building.

No evidence can be found as to whether there was a crane in the goods shed, however, there is clear evidence in official drawings that there was a 1 ½ ton crane in the goods shed at Wylye and as that shed is almost identical, and built at the same time as Wishford then it is reasonable to assume that there was also a 1 ½ ton crane sited on the loading platform inside Wishford Goods Shed.

A standard GWR loading gauge was hung from the Wilton end wall of the goods shed over the rail exit.

Coal

It is relatively clear that the majority of freight dealt with was coal, with at least 3 coal merchants using the site. G M Young (who also owned the Post Office, Shop and Bakery in South Street) appears to have been the main user, he rented (from the GWR), 180 square yards of the site, weighbridge and hut. Edwin Carey from Stapleford was another major user and he rented 80 square yards of the area of the site. In addition to these two the Withers Family from Shrewton took all

The sidings behind the station in the 1930s. Note the Morris 1 Ton Commercial, the registration of which, MW9025 was registered to one of the coal merchants, Edwin Carey, who used the station. Note also the siding in the foreground still having longitudinal sleepering (which was used on broad gauge lines.

their coal from this yard, and it appears there also may have been another coal merchant from the Woodford Valley who also used the yard.

The coal siding appears to have been of such length that it could take some 12 wagons, or so and to the roadside of this siding there were two sections of coal staithes, one 80 foot by 10 foot and the other 40 foot by 10 foot – possibly the larger being used by G M Young and the smaller by Edwin Carey. This siding and the area of coal staithes now forms part of the gardens of Ofre Saet and The Sidings, whilst gardening much coal has been found in the garden of Ofre Saet, mostly from their gateway and along the road boundary.

In the early (broad gauge) days of the line most coal came from the Radstock coalfields, it is evident from much of the very early proposals for the line one of the main uses of the line would be to take coal from Radstock for the ports of Portsmouth and Southampton, this would have entailed transfer to 'narrow gauge wagons in the Transfer Shed at Salisbury.

From the opening of the line Radstock had a coal sidings and the line went directly into Ludlows Colliery, this was soon to be connected to Tynings, Middle Pit and Writhlington Pits. (Chris Handley gives much detail of the coal pits in his books, Radstock Coal and Steam Volumes 1 & 2). Later coal came from many of the South Wales pits and in particular Bullo Pill Pit in the Forest of Dean, Aberdare, Radyr, Bassaleg, Rogerstone and Penarth.

Coal traffic along the line appears to have been the main traffic throughout the life of the station, with most trains emanating from South Wales and stopping at Salisbury for a change from Great Western loco (28xx, 72xx, 52xx, 47xx, 49xx, locos used, if only local traffic from Westbury it may have been a 56xx) to a Southern one for the final part of the journey to the ports, coal being used for naval and merchant ships and some for export. These trains have been reported, in general as at least 40 wagons and brake van but there are occasions of trains of 56 wagons, this being the maximum for the line, on most occasions these trains would be banked from Westbury by a Westbury loco due to the incline at Upton Scudamore.

Timber

W M Chalke of South Newton had much of their timber shipped in to Wishford. As they had outlets and other parts of their business around London there was, in the 1930's, a regular freight service from Paddington at least once a week had destinations of Salisbury and Westbury, but in January 1939 there was a 2250 service from Paddington with wagons for destinations of Wells, Westbury, Taunton and Wishford (one wagon normally) – the Wishford wagons would have been dropped at Westbury and marshaled onto the early morning drop off freight for which the loco would have been a 57xx, 45xx or 56xx stopping at all stations to Salisbury to drop off wagons.

Horses and Cattle

The cattle/horse dock to the south western side, on its own siding, accessed from the up line, could take some 5 horse boxes (GWR codename pacos) and at least one cattle truck. This siding was put in during 1909 and accepted for use by the surveyor on 1 September 1909.

Horse traffic would have come mainly from the Druids Lodge Stables, where the proprietor was A P Cunliffe (see the book Druids Lodge Confederacy for more specific information). It is evident the siding was put in for his use, it was too late for Army for Salisbury Plain as by this time the Amesbury and Bulford Camp Railway had opened and too early for WWI, in any case it was much further away than Bulford or even Devizes. Just how much sway A P Cunliffe had on the building of this siding is unknown. Was his winner of the 1913 Derby, 'Abayer' one of the horses that were taken to the races from here?

After Cunliffe's death in 1942 J V Rank bought Druids Lodge and had his racehorses stabled there until his death in 1953, one of his jockeys was Scobie Breasley from 1950 to 1952.

Two Horse Boxes, No 535 of Lot 437 (Diagram N4) and No 590 of Lot 504 (Diagram N6) were hired from the GWR and written "J V Rank Esq., Druids Lodge, Wilts. Return to Wishford. One definitive movement reported is 535 and 590 returned to Wishford 13 May 1941 – no detail can be obtained from racecourse sources relating to which horses, or racecourses were involved.

Cattle may have come from any of the farms in the vicinity but most probably from Joe Thatcher who had his barns (rented from Wilton Estate) opposite the Post Office in the village, others may have been Manor Farm.

Milk

Between the down line and the coal siding was a small siding, stopping behind the signal box and just before the main station building, this was built for the milk traffic and other items which were put into end loading wagons. Latterly the milk was put onto the early passenger train at approx. 0800 and later in the day at times between 1600 and 1730. Southington Farm at Stapleford regularly used this facility as did Mr. Moore also of Stapleford. This milk was sent to many locations but certainly to Trowbridge and London.

Other known freight

Bricks were brought in, prior to WWII, for Mr. Grant a builder from Stapleford, some of which came from Heinz in Gillingham. Mouldings the local builders who built the stables at Druids Lodge also built at least 12 houses in the village, the bricks for which would have come in by rail. In addition to these the bricks for the houses/bungalows built at Mount Pleasant, Stoford in 1950/51 were brought in by rail, most probably from the Westbury Brick and Tile Pottery Co. at Penleigh, Dilton Marsh.

It is considered sheep may have been transported to markets from here, but no specific reference can be found.

Pigeons were regularly dropped off at the station for either taking to other stations for letting off, but numerous were let off at this station.

Materials for the tennis courts at Shrewton, built just after WWII, at The Recreation Ground were brought in via Wishford, the site of the tennis courts is now the children's play area.

Another item was a Claude Butler sidecar for a Claude Butler Tandem, brought in from London c1949 for George Wells who lived at Orcheston (now living in Stoford).

Many farms in the area obtained their fertilizer from the station.

Private Owner wagons recorded on line:
Denaby
Kilmersdon & Writhlington Colleries
The Fife Coal
Aston
Westbury Iron Works
Clarke Lush & Co. (Salisbury)
Somerset Collieries
Read & Sons (Salisbury)
Badbury
Burr &~ Gibbons
WAC

Phillips & Co
C.W.S. London
John Simm & Co Ltd
Hayward& Barton Coal Merchants
Bedwas Coke
Dunkerton Coal Factors
AAC Anthracite
Dunkerton Collieries
This is not a definitive list of all PO wagons that could have been seen, it is merely a listing of those identified from photographs and other research.

Military Use
Between 1897 and 1900 the Military had started to purchase lands on Salisbury Plain for manoeuvres and camps were being set up. Mid summer 1900 saw the first large influx of troop movements for training and although Military Railways had been proposed and accepted, the Light Railway Order for the Amesbury and Military Camp Railway was granted on the 28 September 1898 and opened on 1 October 1901, and the extension to Bulford on 1 June 1906.

Westdown Camp (near Tilshead) opened on 14 July 1900 and the first regiments, some 4500 men, were The Severn Brigade comprising of 2nd and 3rd Somerset Light Infantry, 1st Gloucestershire Regiment, 3rd Welch Regiment and 3rd Glamorganshire Rifle Volunteers. Attached to these were the 1st East Yorkshire Regiment and 1st York and Lancashire Regiment (Hallamshire Rifle Volunteers). The latter are reported being entrained at Sheffield Midland Station to Wishford and had to march the 9 miles, or so, to that camp (via Stapleford, Berwick St James and Shrewton), and they returned via the same route. The Times reports "We are requested to report that Devizes Station is three miles nearer to West Down Camp than any other station. Wishford is a remote village siding a great deal further off."

No details can be found regarding which station the Severn Brigade used but the large volume of troops would need large trains and these would have been put into sidings such that normal train services could be run whilst these army units were disembarking from their special trains.

During WWII and mainly during the very latter years there were American Forces (USAF 1925, 1927, 1929 Ordenance Company Aviation Combat Support Wing) stationed in Grovely Woods at Ammunition Dumps (AAF592) (they were

5969 Honington Hall heads the 1037 Cardiff to Portsmouth passenger on 1/11/1937.

supported by 2133rd Aviation Engineer Firefighting Platoon), it appears that they used the sidings for some incoming and outgoing supplies, but they more regularly used Wylye as these sidings had been radically extended specifically for this purpose. It has been reported the American Forces assisted in transporting a tractor and a thresher to one of the local farms from the station and it is distinctly possible these may have formed part of the lend lease agreement.

During WWII the Home Guard suggested 'The enemy objective is unlikely to be Wishford or other villages, but the railway, telephone communications and military installations may be considered vunerable'.

In Wishford Home Guard information it indicated B White and W Gane were labourors for digging, demolition and rescue "if free from railway duties". In many small village locations one of the duties of the Home Guard was to guard the railway line by patrolling the line and in particular the station and goods areas.

It has been reported the signal box was used as a lookout station during this period.

The line saw regular Ambulance trains which were hauled either by LNER B12's or GWR 63xx.

Accidents

There was only one accident at Wishford: The Winchester and Salisbury Journal reports:

On 20 August 1874 a special cattle train, which left Bristol at 3.55, travelling to Salisbury, collided with a trolley just outside Wishford, the trolley heading towards Wylye. Four men were on the trolley and as a result of the accident two brothers names Smith, and a Richard Simper were all injured. The other man, George West, of Wilton, died at the site of the accident. The men had taken the trolley without permission and had been assisting a local farmer, Mr. Galpin (a farmer at Little Langford), with his harvesting, and were unaware of the special cattle train (despite it being shown in timetables as 'runs when required every other Monday'). The engine and train were undamaged and the crew not injured but the trolley was smashed to atoms. The inquest held at Wyle on 21 August 1874 stated they had no right to use the trolley and that the company (Great Western Railway) were not at all to blame and a verdict of 'Accidental Death' was recorded. It should be noted that this is the second report of an accident concerning this 'special cattle train', the other being at Salisbury Station on 6 October 1856.

The Warminster Herald of 22 August 1874 reports:

"Wishford – Fatal Accident on the railway.

The village was thrown into a state of great and painful excitement on Thursday night when it became known that some packers had met with an accident on the line, and that one of them had lost his life. The facts of the case may be briefly stated. A number of men had been working near Wishford Station. Work was suspended at the usual hour, and the ganger had the trawley that was used occasionally when the line was clear locked up, as was his duty. George West, Richard Simpson, George Smith, and Oliver Smith, who had all been employed on the line, in fact were regular packers, had some harvest work to do near Wylye, so they managed to procure a key and unlock the trawley, which they placed on the line and went away at a spanking pace. After they had done their work they proceeded back on the trawley to Wishford, and a very short distance the Wylye side of Wishford they were overtaken by a special cattle train proceeding to Salisbury at the rate of 25 miles an hour. The train dashed into the trawley, and smashed it to pieces, killing George West, and severely injuring the other three, who were speedily as possible conveyed to Salisbury Infirmary, where they, of course received the best surgical treatment. Simpson and George Smith has each had a limb amputated, and Oliver Smith has received, it is feared, an injury to his spine, while they are all three otherwise much bruised and shaken. It seems almost like a miracle that they were not all killed. The accident took place at about 10 minutes to 9 o'clock, when it was nearly dark. That the men on the trawley did not hear the train approaching them is to be accounted for by the noise that the trawley made, and their attention being taken up with propelling of the trawley. They were also ignorant of the fact that any train was timed to pass at that time, or of course they would not have been foolish enough to run the risk, and that the driver of the cattle train did not perceive any obstruction on the line is to be attributed to the fact it was nearly dark, and a little curve in the line must also have obstructed the view till the train was nearly up to the trawley. If the engine driver had perceived the obstruction he would have sounded his whistle, and the unfortunate men might have had time to stumble off the trawley. No part of the train was damaged nor was the shock sufficient to injure the driver and others in charge, of it. It should be stated that though these packers did not know that a special cattle train had been put on, the Company's servants had all received due notice of it, and had, of course, kept the line clear. An inquest was held at Wishford yesterday, on the body of George West, who was 46 years of age. Chief Inspector Liddiard, of Bristol, and Inspector Morrison, of Trowbridge were in attendance on behalf of the Great Western Railway Company, and rendered every assistance in their power for the through elucidation of the truth. The facts as above stated were proved in evidence, and as it was clear the men were trespassers on the line at the time, the jury had no difficulty in arriving at a verdict, which was ;Accidental death'. They also completely exonerated the company's servants from blame."

N.B. In the above report the paper has incorrectly reported one name – Robert Simpson is incorrect and should read 'Richard Simper', who appears to have lived at South Newton.

It is considered that the trolley was only at Wishford for the purpose of completion of Gauge Conversion work as this accident occurs only 2 months after that conversion.

Although not classed as an 'accident' there have been 2 incidents reported, at Wishford, where couplings parted on trains.

Other Accidents between Salisbury and Westbury: 6 October 1856 – a special cattle train ran into Salisbury Terminus Station at speed killing one driver and one fireman and over 100 sheep; 5 August 1873 at Skew Bridge Salisbury between a Goods Train and a Passenger Train. 1 driver died, 1 driver injured and both firemen injured plus injuries to at least 10 passengers; 2 September 1916 at Warminster between two passenger trains. 1 passenger died and 12 were injured.

There have also been numerous reports in local papers of injuries to 'persons' on the line, some involving trains, but none reported at Wishford.

Other Use of Land

Many Great Western stations allowed staff to use parts of the land for their own use, usually as an allotment, during the early 1930's Edmund West was allowed use of land between the up platform and the cattle dock for poultry runs and for a pigeon coop. His father Edmund Charles West was also a pigeon fancier and lived in Ashley Road, Salisbury – both father and son got a number of their pigeons from another fancier, and breeder, in Avon Terrace, Salisbury. Pigeons regularly flew between these three locations and if any were found to be missing they were generally at one of these three locations. It is clear from later photographs these chicken runs were still being used, possibly, right up to closure of the station in 1955.

CHAPTER 7
USE OF LAND AFTER CLOSURE

T he site of Wishford Station in 2010.No evidence of the original station or platforms can be seen, only Station House (formerly Station Masters House) remains. The new housing built on the old railway land consists of: Green Haven, Ofre Saet, Sidings, Weathertop. After closure in 1955 the land previously occupied by the sidings (on the main station platform side) has been

The site of Wishford Station in 2010. No evidence of the original station or platforms can be seen, only Station House (formerly Station Master's House) remains.

built on with new houses, the only remaining structure that is still intact is the Station Master's House (now called Station House).

The bungalow Green Haven (built c1980) is built in what was the garden of the Station House and looks down on the line; the end of the platform and footbridge would have been almost alongside where this property is built.

The bungalow Ofre Saet (also built c1980) is built almost immediately in front of the original station building where its driveway would have been the station approach and car park. In the rear garden there is a raised flower bed which may possibly have been the edge of the platform to the right of the station building, also in this area and close to the current garage is a wet patch in the garden which may have been either a water supply to the station building or part of the drain system from the station toilets. Also in the rear garden there is what appears to be a drain cover and this would have been just to the rear of the station building. To the front of the property would have been the siding which was used by the coal merchants, very much evidence of this has been found very close to the roadside boundary and to a depth of some 3 feet where coal has been dug up during gardening. After the railway lines were taken up it is evident the site was not 'totally' cleared as a short piece of railway line has been dug up in this garden.

To the left of the property would have been where the short siding, used for milk churns, was located.

The bungalow The Sidings, built approx 1993, by Gorringe, is situated almost behind where the Signal Box stood and on the bed of the siding leading to the goods shed and the one for coal.

The bungalow Weathertop, built 1993 by Gorringe, is situated just to the station side of the site of the goods shed. The goods shed would have taken up most of the back garden.

It has been reported that a previous builder submitted planning applications for a residence either as a conversion of the goods shed or on the footprint of the goods shed, this application was not turned down by the Salisbury Council Planning Department but by British Railways.

The Up Line Sidings area (horse and cattle dock) are partially used by Network Rail for track access and partially privately owned containing a number of disused buildings, formerly a small holding. The 1970's track re-alignment moved both running tracks to alleviate the curvature and the up line now forms part of what was the cattle and horse dock siding.

ABOUT THE AUTHOR

Terry Waldron was born in the small village of Minety in 1948 and like many children of that era had the obligatory Hornby clockwork train set. The initial fascination for love of steam came from travelling between the village and Swindon regularly on a Saturday either for shopping or to support Swindon Town FC. Like many boys of that time he wanted to work on the railway, preferably as a train driver, this was not to be so as steam was in its decline as was the works at Swindon.

He almost always had some form of train set or model railway, even though this was not avidly pursued during the early years of marriage. But this was further pursued in modelling in O Gauge for many years.

His first ventures into research was to assist Paul Burkhalter for his book on Devonport Dockyard Railway. This was followed by carrying out research into canal boats that were part of the Ellesmere Port Boat Museum collection.

ALSO AVAILABLE IN THIS SERIES

The Lambourn Valley Railway
Great Wishford Station
More to follow soon.

See our full range of railway books on the History Page of our website
www.bretwaldabooks.com